To Tiffany,

Forever grateful for
the gift of your person and
friendship, forever in awe
of your person and friendship,
forever looking up to you.
So much love and then some
more,

Deu
04/01
(a book I picked
up for you in
New Orleans)

THE LAST CEREMONY

Susan Deer Cloud

FootHills Publishing

ACKNOWLEDGMENTS

Some of the poems in this volume originally appeared in the following anthologies: *Sister Nations, Native American Women Writers on Community*; *Low Explosions, Writings on the Body*; *Ladyfest*East 2004*; *Ugly People, Beautiful Poems*; *Rhetorical Visions, Writing & Reading in a Visual Culture*.

And other of these poems first appeared in *Rosebud*; *Earth's Daughters*; *Prairie Schooner*; *Identity Theory*; *Paterson Literary Review*; *Pembroke Magazine, Native American Literature (Tribute to Vine Deloria, Jr., Issue)*; *Shenandoah (Native American Issue)*; *Chiron Review*; *The Bridge*; *Word Weavings*; *Negative Capability*; *Akwe:kon, a Journal of Indigenous Issues*; *Earth Tones; Poetry International/Abani: Indigenous Issue*; *Poets Against the War Website*.

"The Dirt in the Gallery across from the Old Whorehouse on State Street" received Honorable Mention in 2004 Allen Ginsberg Poetry Competition. "Welcome to the Land of Ma'am" received *Prairie Schooner's* Readers' Choice Award in 2003. "You Really Have" received 3rd Prize in *Chiron Review's* 1999 Poetry Contest. "Vincent Van Gogh Writes to Madame Calment from the Stars" received 2nd Prize in *Negative Capability's* 1999 Poetry Competition.

***

Drawing on page 85
"Raven/Self-Portrait" by Andy Hill

Cover art, *Indian Women on Trail of Tears*, is by Danielle Hauptfleisch.

ISBN: 0-941053-99-7

FootHills Publishing
P. O. Box 68
Kanona, NY 14856
www.foothillspublishing.com

"If we fight we are too few. If we die we are too many."
Mohawk Chief Tiyanoga (a.k.a. King Hendrick)

"A nation is not defeated until its women's hearts are on the ground."
From the Cheyenne Nation ...

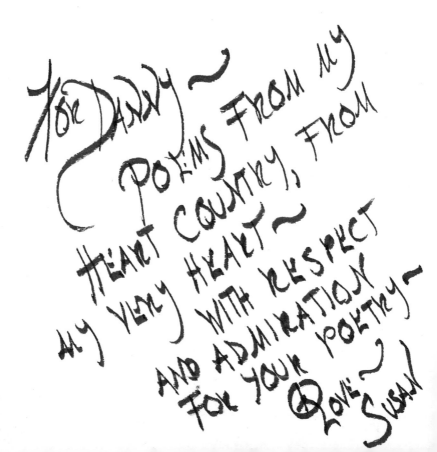

FOR

My sister, Erelene, who is not only a "blood" sister to me but a spirit sister who shares my heart song.

Barbara Mann (Seneca) & Libby Tucker (Eastern Cherokee), beautiful, kind, and brilliant friends who kept making a stand for me during the times I could hardly even crawl anymore.

William Meyers (Eastern Cherokee), *one good Indian man.* For your Bear Medicine, for what you did at the fire for me.

Ben Buddha, Word Warrior of the Stars, who grew his hair out long for me in the old way, who led me off my Trail of Tears onto a Bridge of Smiles.

Marie McKenna, goddess of Lost Dog Café, wise woman, easy laugher, who in the old Irish way keeps a candle burning for any stranger, poet, Christ, angel out in the rain.

My brothers, Joseph, John, and Daniel, men of great warm heart who make me proud.

CONTENTS

MARLON BRANDO DIES AT 80

It blasts me when I open AOL Instant Messenger,
which flashes current news before I pop up my Buddy List.
Right now I wish I could IM you, Marlon, thank you for
hating Hollywood and for bugging America's low carb liberals
by getting fat on Big Macs after you buttered that actress
in "Last Tango in Paris" with the real thing, no *I can't believe
it's not butter* for you, and pissing off conservative Indian haters,
closet and otherwise, by sending Sacheen Littlefeather to 1973
Academy Awards – black-haired Apache princess refusing
Oscar for you. And thanks for kissing Larry King on the lips,
for playing the trickster. In the article, Marlon, they refer to
your brutal male beauty. I know what they mean. I have watched
"A Streetcar Named Desire" more times than I can count
on my "ten little Indian" fingers that yearned to hold your naked
body hot to the campfire of my nakedness even after you got
anti-beautiful people fat. Marlon, I loved you. Up there
on the big screen, I wanted to suck that sultry scowl of mouth
on the verge of kiss from the time I was a girl. You made me
feel like a multi-orgasmic woman even then.

MARLON BRANDO DIES AT 80. My brother, you will never die.
Once a sister and I got into a discussion about you and Mel Gibson
when other women were wetting their polyester thongs
over Aussie-man. Macho Mel, buff, blue-eyed – all the women
had seen him in "Braveheart," imagining him fundamental
beneath his kilts. The sister said, "I would still take Brando fat
over Mel skinny any day." I said, "So would I." And we laughed,
ecstatic. *Brutal?* Those critics don't get what we talked about.
Marlon, we knew your real beauty, something deep down
crying, tender, and so sensitive-crazy that no old age or obesity
or people's stupidity could rob it from you. Marlon, they can say
you died, but you are alive in this Indian heart, you are a part
of Indian territory because somehow you were of our heartbreak,
of our love medicine, of our forever crying for a vision no matter
how much the white man stole our land, our language, our traditions,
no matter how many children died, how many of us drank ourselves
to suicide. We all saw it in your listening eyes,

the young, black-haired, broken nosed man with his glistening
warrior's glance. Marlon, I offer you the wild rose sweetness
of my desire, the smiles of my people before Columbus came,
our hearts that break yet keep round dancing back into song.
Brando, I offer you this poetry. Brother, I send you
with blessing and grace into the Spirit World where
my grandfathers and my grandmothers greet you.

HALF-BREED AT TEN YEARS OLD, THE GREAT DEPRESSION

When teacher gave us children our school pictures
I stared out the window at winter trees. Not
that I feared I'd look ugly, because already
I'd been praised as *pretty* past any number
I ever counted to. People said it was my eyes,
color they called *grey*. When they flattered me
I thanked them, as Mother had taught me
to be very polite. When boys praised me,
my shy skin flamed campfire red,
remembered the words *Red Indian*.
No, it wasn't that kind of ugly I feared.

It was what could betray my face, that mix
of *lady*, my mother, marrying *Indian*, my father.
It was knowing that the Indian was wild, not so much
when he dragged home from working as a stone mason
from sunrise to dusk, but who he became after
he ate, bathed, donned his best clothes, drove off
to gamble in cellars and alleyways. In his absence
Mother taught my sisters and me how to walk, speak,
sit like *ladies*. The demure dresses she sewed for us
came with a warning: *Stay away from wild boys with wind-
combed hair and eyes the hue of seventh Heaven.*

It was my father's blue eyes that I feared
when finally I uncovered with shaking hands
my multiple faces inside thin paper that made me feel
as if I were touching the translucent skin of my dreams
hungering to fly away each night, sing my father home to us.
Would my face tattle-tell on me, hint I wasn't who I tried
to pass as but an Indian girl worth less than caked mud
on my schoolmates' boots? Wasn't it bad enough to crave
food every minute of the day, search cracked sidewalks
for dropped dimes, work a pencil down to its nub,
unable to buy a new one? Wasn't it bitter enough
to learn so young never to ask for seconds?

I clutched the largest picture in my left hand, hand
the teachers used to tie to my chair so I wouldn't keep
coloring with it, be of the Devil when I grew up.
Around me the other children were laughing, pleased
by their faces captured flat like that. My eyes
stung as though filled with tears, yet were dry.
They gazed half-starved into the 8 x 10's opaque eyes
dreaming between long, straight bangs and quizzical
glint of smile. Seneca. Wolf eyes. Grey.
Beneath my flowered dress I crossed my legs
bowed by rickets, feeling the rub
of blushing thighs.

I slid my face back between the soft
paper, the *lady* my mother raised me to be,
the *half-breed* howling mutely
for her blue-eyed father.

HER POCAHONTAS

"Why will you take by force what you may have quietly by love?"
Powhatan, father of Pocahontas

Her Pocahontas was a doll given to her by her mother.
Her Pocahontas was an earth-skinned, dark-haired, amber-eyed baby
pressed into her three-year-old arms starting to reach past infancy
and innocence. "This doll's name is Pocahontas," her mother said.
"This doll is Indian like me. This doll is Indian like you.
Take good care of her. Hold her close to your heart."

Her Pocahontas was the most her mother ever said about being Indian.
It was the 1950s. People had secrets. People kept silent.
No one talked about it, and the children didn't know why.
Her Pocahontas was a soft, sad darkness who couldn't cry,
whose eyes never closed, who had an invisible tongue.
Her Pocahontas liked to be sung to deep in the forest.

Her Pocahontas was nothing like the dolls the other girls had.
Their dolls were Christmas presents with blue eyes, curly blonde hair,
petite plastic noses. Their dolls would never need nose jobs or smell
fear. Their dolls had eyes that shut so they wouldn't have to take
everything in. Their dolls cried fake tears. They made an awful
whining sound if you turned them upside-down.

Her Pocahontas was Indian. The other girls played house with dolls
that had skin like refined sugar for baking cakes. They expected
their dolls to grow up, to be like the actresses they worshipped
on vast movie screens – blonde, pug-nosed Doris Day always
"holding out," golden, pout-lipped Marilyn hinting with winks
she "put out." Her Pocahontas had Technicolor visions in the woods.

Her Pocahontas was a doll with a short life expectancy.
Her Pocahontas was a baby who knew better than to cry. No one
talked about it, but there was an unspoken memory of soldiers
and death. Her Pocahontas had a body dark as night, undomesticated
as stars, naked as dreams. The other girls hated her Pocahontas.
They had their own Pocahontas, a confection of lies.

13

Their Pocahontas had two white Johns and became white herself.
Their Pocahontas was a fantasy that popped up on medicine bottles,
cigar lids and butter boxes. Their Pocahontas was a film star, first
a squaw saving the White Man in bad cowboy-and-Indian movies, last
a buckskin-Barbie disguised by Disney as politically correct.
Any girl could be one. Her Pocahontas knew the truth
but couldn't speak.

When her mother died too young, her eldest brother asked her
after the funeral, "Whatever happened to that doll Ma gave you –
Pocahontas?" She stood there in the whirling snow, cradling
darkness close to her heart, and couldn't remember.
"Maybe," she told him, "she died of smallpox, of arms and legs
broken for trying to bring back the old dances, of a tongue slit
for speaking her own language."

Her Pocahontas was a doll given to her by her dead mother.

SUZY DOLL

We stop at Deming Museum, break from New Mexico highway,
cars hurtling 90 miles per hour through desert air. I had been flying
with the rest of them when I spotted the sign advertising Anasazi pottery
and *other ancient Indian things*. I was ready to dream mesa designs,
lightning and ravens, half abstract deer, spirals of stillness.
Manifest Destiny's great granddaughter who grabs our money past
Museum door, hustles us into an unexpected room, a Toy Museum.
She points out a Japanese doll, serene face scorched on left jaw, one eye
sliced. While the woman babbles, I read the card at kimono's red hem:
This doll was found in the rubble by Warren Kollach after the bombing
of Hiroshima (8/6/45). He put her under his coat and returned to his ship.
I read the doll's name. *Suzy.*

The woman is laughing happily now. "The doll's hair would have
been cut from the woman whose daughter was given the doll,
a Japanese custom. The soldier who snuck the doll from Hiroshima
wasn't supposed to – radiation, you know. The night watchman
claims that late at night Suzy glows in the dark." My tongue thickens,
mushrooms at the back of my throat until I barely can breathe. I stare
at this doll with my name, its face serious as my child's face,
flash back to that post World War II girl I was, and to my father
blasted through his chest on Guam – how I used to ask if he had killed
any Japanese, wondered if there were daughters like me crying
fatherless on the other side of the Pacific. He'd chant, "I don't think
I killed anyone, I don't think so." I'd continue playing with corals,
conchs, cowries he brought home in mason jars for his unborn children,

but there were days I overheard him speak that word, "Hiroshima,"
listened to it flower like a white gardenia from his mouth and other
veterans' mouths : "The bombing won the war, saved thousands
of lives." Now I hear my husband tell the white woman that *his wife*
has the same name as the doll, that *his wife Suzy* is Indian, reason
he was dragged to this Museum. I hear him thinking he is witty.
"Oh," the docent giggles, "I thought Indians in the East were all dead."
I clench hands, teeth, my very heart – try not to imagine what happened
to the Japanese girl who never got to grow up as I did, try not to feel
her first happy surprise at the silk gardenia of light flashing

above her and her mother – not to wince at how tight she hugged
the doll in its flowered kimono and mother's hair when colors
turned black, skin seared off bone, bone burned
to shadow.

I glance at the woman's permed hair dyed bombshell blonde,
her doll-like dress, her seventy year old cheerleader's voice
still dominating the world – and at my domineering husband
whose radiated prostate cancer is rooting inside his bones
like tiny gardenias, only he doesn't know it yet. Nor do I
suspect he is going to try to destroy me before he dies,
the hatred of the *squaw* that was there all along finally metastasized.
"Yeah, " I say, my face glowing *unsmiling* as my child's face,
the doll's face, "funny the way the dead always manage
to find each other."

WELCOME TO THE LAND OF MA'AM

Welcome to The Land of Ma'am, where countless Indians
perished because brazen, young invaders erected
their "Land of the Free" on Turtle Island, Mother Earth.
Welcome to The Land of Ma'am, where you are free
to be young, smooth-skinned, strong – free to call women with silver
gracing their long hair *Ma'am*. Welcome, you who stand indifferent
as the godlike models in *Vanity Fair*, you GAP boys with bulges
of retro-testosterone in your khaki pants, addressing women like me
in John Wayne drawls, *Excuse me, Ma'am*, if you see us at all. Welcome
to moon-drawn decades of walking on Earth, to wise-woman hair,
to faces carved with petroglyph-wrinkles, myths in flesh.

And welcome, you who are young and female, blonde and glittering
with rings in noses, ears, tongues – you who are pricked
with bold tattoos on the drunken dough of derrières bouncing
like rap music beneath the hip hop of high skirts. To you, especially,
welcome to The Land of Ma'am, girls serving me in restaurants, stores,
so confident your waists will never expand, nor black witch hairs sprout
on your chins overnight, nor the charmed cells of tinsel-town behinds
migrate like disoriented geese to your anorexic arms. *Ma'am,
do you need help?* The nasal riptide of a sneer undercuts
your deodorized *ma'ams*. Oh, doomed Lolitas of America's malls,
Ophelias of the Big Mac born with the silver spoons of Hollywood lies
up rhinoplastic noses, playing bad girls, cracking into mad girls when
you can't pretend you're perfect products anymore –
welcome to that land you're destined for.

Welcome to The Land of Ma'am, where the old grow invisible
inside "The Land of the Free." Welcome to the reservation
that the young, the powerful, the rich try to consign you to,
as if you were a cast-off dress with no body in it, fit only
for a thrift shop, mothballed purview of the poor. And welcome
to the end of sex, where "Wham, bam, thank you, Ma'am" shrivels
into new meaning – no bodies over twenty allowed in this America
of TV-programmed Crest-white teeth, Jane Fonda-implant breasts,
contact lens-throw away-blue eyes, collagen-smiles, sucked-thin thighs.

Who would want to make love to decades of daydreams, longing,
sorrow, ecstasy, delicate wisdom glowing like wildflowers
in moonlight – want to kiss flesh like hills warmed by many suns,
gullied by stinging rains, hypnotic snows? Welcome to the land
of mammograms.

I say Ma'ams of the World unite, start your own goddess-business!
I say make "Ban the Ma'am" buttons, then wear them proudly
on red tee-shirts, your breasts soft and low and braless underneath!
Every chance you get, thrust out buttons of defiance on street corners,
at malls, universities, movie houses, banks, the halls of Congress, yes!
Ma'ams, snatch back this land and don't plead "*pretty pleeease!*"
Dream it the way it was before the tribes were divided, crushed,
when older women were revered as beautiful elders, medicine women,
wise women, beloved women, when the People cried for their visions
in the female heart of the ancient hills.

Ma'ams, it's a good day to die.

YOU REALLY HAVE

balls, for years the boys and then all the men
in my life tossed me their highest compliment.
For years, beginning with those first, fierce seasons
when I was a tomboy with Genghis Khan eyes, bloodied knees,
hair that refused to grow, I accepted their praise
like glass beads my Mohawk and Blackfoot ancestors
accepted from long ago white men. *You have big balls,*
my brothers, boy cousins, boyfriends draped and decorated me
with their hot words whenever I stole golden apples for them
from the private orchards at street's end, or disobeyed
my mother and stole far into the woods behind the house,
or played hooky from the public school that stank
of institutionalized wax and scrubbed brains, bearing my renegade
body up to the high mountaintops, seeking my instruction
in caves, meadows, trees. When I grew older, finally sprouting
hair and even breasts, my older, educated lovers further
enlightened me, *You really have cojones*, as we played at Hemingway,
struggling to create our own code out of the confusion of present wars —
war in Vietnam, war against Blacks, war against women, Indians, poets,
the poor, the broken "mad," and the final nuclear war against
the whirling, exuberant cells of our naked bodies.

For years I was so proud, swaggering down city streets
with brazen balls, unafraid, smuggling my glass beads, smile,
and Indian love medicine into America's ghettos at high noon,
or riding barefooted up elevators to skyscraper tops, peering out
over oceanic nighttime lights, high tides of shine and shimmer,
gold and silver, or sneaking into city parks after closing clock time,
crouching like a ghost with my phantom cojones, surrounded by
memories of ancestors in the tamed remnants of ancient forest,
all around me like a tightening noose countless millions of the living
sleeping, or trying to sleep, in their coffin-rooms. *Why don't you
or I ever get mugged?*, I once asked my schizophrenic friend, Irish Larry,
as we watched the sun set on our off-white skins in the heart of Harlem.
Look at us, he cried. *They see our balls. They see you, a woman, know you*

*possess cojones, wild, potent, polysyllabic cojones. They think we're going
to mug them!"* And I was so proud, so fearless, as our skins turned
Bessie Smith-dark with the falling sun.

You really have balls, for too many years my ex-husband
lavished me with his vodka cocktail-praise, having to have me
because he saw me stride free down Liberty, New York, streets,
blowing love notes through Indian flute into spring air, sweeping
dirty sidewalks with torn dress hems, trying to liberate parrots
and canaries caged like rainbows in the Five-and-Dime he managed.
I could have you arrested, he warned when he caught me fiddling
with the latches and bars. *But since you have such big you know whats
(for a woman), will you go out to dinner with me?* The rest
was cowboys and Indians all over again, white man against red
woman, days and nights of drunken fights determining just who
was going to win this war. And I was buried in balls —
boob tube ball games — my ex-husband, former glory boy
of high school football, baseball, softball, soccer ball, cheering
every conceivable ball thrown, hit, kicked, punched
across the stupefying screen. When I fought him, all those balls
and all that boredom, he said, *You're so sexy when you're mad,*
and, *Oooo,* then we'd ball in bed.

O tempores, o cojones, what was I, a young wife, to do, but read
radical feminist literature, drop in to college, get back to my Native
roots by writing poetry, return in secret to the deep woods?

For years the boys and then all the men in my life
tossed a lariat of praise around my neck, roped me in.
I loved them for it. I loved them for helping me be so proud.
But these days whenever some blue-eyed songster hotly breathes,
You really have balls, I think, *No, I really have cunt.*
*So did my mother, her mother before her, and all the women
blood-rivering back to the original wise woman whose glowing ovum
resulted in me. All the loving, laughing, dignified, healing,
singing dreamers who slipped through the endless Burning Times,
bequeathing a legacy of dreamer-women to Mother Earth.*

I laugh at the songsters, realizing that for years the compliments
from all the boys and men were nothing but a way for them
with their silently clanging balls to get where they most longed
to be, inside my cunt, inside the juicy, blackberry mystery of cosmic
cunt, of goddess-fire, passion-screams, a time outside time
more ancient than star-come. Now whenever any sweet man
smelling of heady, musty cologne, invisible pheromones, tosses me
his ultimate compliment, *You really have a lot of balls*, I pitch him
my ultimate compliment right back — *You really have
a lot of cunt.*

OLD MAN

The last winter she lived in that house
a prehistoric looking bug appeared
on walls she and her husband
painted jonquil yellow.

By then November's hatch
of ladybugs had disappeared.
She was missing them until that bug
stared down at her one night

when she was washing dishes,
staring out into the woods.
He waved his antennae in a dance
at her from above the window,

while she swayed there feeling strangely
happy, soap suds crackling in tiny rainbows
across her tired hands. She imagined
that was the end of the affair

but that bug hung out in the kitchen
all winter, crawling from wall to wall
and across the yellow mesa of ceiling.
She really liked him. She liked his body

with its legs like sticks and the whole
weird thing looking like dirt when it ceased
moving. After awhile she was pretty sure
he was speaking to her with the antennae,

some kind of code talk. She named him
Old Man, opportunity to tell
her leftover hippie friends, "I really dig
my Old Man." As for the husband,

they no longer painted anything bright.
One night – no Old Man waving
over the sink. By then she had lifted
her hands out of the soap water,
had let those rainbows fly,

and if she has one regret
it is that she never kissed Old Man
beneath his antennae to see if it was like
the fairy tales after all, the happily
ever after, the ugliness turned into beauty.

WONDER BREAD (for Ben Buddha)

That spring she took up eating Wonder Bread after years
of buying bread her hypochondriac ex-husband insisted was good
for her — multi-grain bread, sugar-free pitas, honeyed breads
from health food stores. But everyone knows when a wife leaves
a man whose honeyed lies leave her with no choice
except "not putting up with it" anymore, she will become poorer
than her betrayer. Crucified by nails of "put-down" in a house
that never was *her* home, she finally took up resurrection
with a young poetry man. Yes, they were poor, decided to split
rent, make love, write poetry forever in their garret rooms.
When she realized she could no longer afford the expensive breads
of her spent marriage, her lover told her Wonder Bread
was his favorite. He especially liked to eat it with Peter Pan
peanut butter and strawberry jelly. "But it's white bread," she groaned.
"Haven't you heard that expression, *white bread rich?*"
"Wonder Bread is ghetto bread," her lover, whose father begged
for bread in Korea, hugged her to his hairless chest. "Wonder Bread
is the people's bread — the wounded people who learn
to sing, dance, paint from hunger." He began whirling her slowly
across the kitchen floor. Dancing, she remembered the first bread
she ever ate — Wonder Bread. She told her poetry man how such bread
appeared on the porch each morning when she was a girl —
Wonder Bread in polka dot wrapping — eggs from Catskill farms —
milk in glass bottles that clinked like chimes in her still dreaming hands
when she lifted them up. "I felt intrigued by the red, yellow, blue
circles of the see-through bag — begged my mother into making me a
polka dot dress that still exists in the sole studio photograph shot of me."
Whirling, dancing, kissing, she thinks maybe she always understood
something about how everything moves in circles, round dancing
with her lover back to post-War 1950s when her mother and father
were young, poor, romantic and desperate, *she* too small to understand.
That very day she drove to the Giant, bought Wonder Bread,
Peter Pan peanut butter, Smucker's strawberry jelly. That night
she and her uncombed poet picnicked on garret floor, dipping
fingers into jars like grails, tasting home,
eating Wonder.

HARVEST

Lily-Lacks-an-Indian-Name drove country roads
to Conservation Center's Harvest Festival. The Director
had invited Iroquois people from the Nations
to sell arts and crafts and set up teaching booths.
Lily-Lacks-an-Indian-Name liked it on that mountain
where the Center was, sometimes roamed its woods
and river banks when she missed home.

Congress had named November *Native American Month*.
Lily-Lacks-an-Indian-Name wondered "Why"
as she wandered through the Center,
admiring reservation Indians' beadwork,
carved deer antlers, soapstone warriors,
dream catchers that never seemed to catch
good dreams.

Lily-Lacks-an-Indian-Name heard a white boy
shooting questions at an Indian man standing
by ancient arrowheads in a booth for teaching
Iroquois history. She recognized the man
from past powwows, a brother Mohawk.
The boy looked about ten, owning the world
in designer clothes.

What were the Indians like?
How did they make arrowheads?
What did they shoot? Did the Indians
enjoy scalping people?

Lily-Lacks-an-Indian-Name noticed
the Mohawk man whose name she didn't know
go still inside his flannel shirt and jeans,
listened to his "play dead" voice answering
to this boy herding him and her and other
Indian people into the reservations
of past tense.

Yes, Lily-Lacks-an-Indian-Name knew by heart
this scene. She stood there soft as the man's voice,
watched him rendered invisible – blue eyes,
light skin, short hair, no beads, no feathers
decorating his limbs, and that boy striding
happily away with his new knowledge
of dead Indians.

Lily-Lacks-an-Indian-Name tried to make her own
questions soar like arrowheads off her shy tongue.
Why didn't you tell that kid you are Indian?
Why didn't you shout that we are not all ghosts?
Why did you have to be kind enough to let him dance off
with his romance of warriors in eagle feather war bonnets,
his clichés of flying tomahawks and red war paint?

Lily-Lacks-an-Indian-Name gazed at nameless
Mohawk brother studying her in fox way
of Indian men when they decide to look into a woman.
She watched him travel her green eyes, skin no longer
tanned from summer's sun, dress not buckskin, body
crying beneath her coat. She watched him arrive.
Is this woman Indian?

Yes, it was Native American Month,
Harvest of Shame.

TEAR

(Iron Eyes Cody, second generation Italian-American,
played the Indian in 1971 Earth Day spot)

After Sixties' "movements," Vietnam War, assassinations,
we crash-landed in early 'Seventies. Everyone was learning
how to make a fist out of a stunned heart, to raise a voice.
Amerika kept blossoming with unruly roses of psychedelic song,
peace signs, free love, hair everywhere. Black became beautiful,
ladies became feminists, students became hippies, mystics, wild-eyed
radicals. Then there was us, the Indians, staring at the flower children
flaunting beads and feathers the boarding schools stole from
our grandparents. If we weren't in Vietnam, drunk or bleeding
from our wrists, we sat watching it all happen on TV like everyone else.
Other than re-runs of cowboy-and-Indian movies, nothing seemed
to be happening with us. We were so invisible most whites thought
we Eastern Indians flew the way of passenger pigeons.

On the second Earth Day, 1971, we saw an ad against pollution.
Long-haired Indian paddling canoe up polluted river, past factories
to garbage-strewn bank. This Indian strode out of our past
to super highway, trash bag flew from passing car, burst
at his moccasined feet. Tear rolled down his ravaged cheek:
"People start pollution; people can stop it." On that March day
we looked into each other's faces that in secret had wept such tears,
and we didn't say it yet out loud but we thought the same thing,
that maybe we had made it, that maybe we were coming back
like this Indian in his braids and Eagle feather, that maybe now
we could let them see we weren't wooden
but wept like everyone else.

FIRST TIME (for Ben)

You didn't tell me it was your first time. When you bowed
your face to mine and I felt a thousand tiny moth feathers
brush my cheek's inflamed wings, it became my first time, too.
Yet my flesh had known this giddy ride – trembled
from its rapture-rise until all my atoms cloud-danced
into iridescent howl. That Ides-of-March evening we cradled
each other inside the madness that had become Manhattan,
waited in snake dance line to fly up Empire State Building's
erect core. We rose inside the greatest dick-waving skyscraper
in the Milky Way, packed in with elevator-strangers –
"What if" flapping crow-like across claustrophobic eyes.
"What if terrorists decide to aim planes into what is
once more the longest building in this city where
if you can make it here you can make it anywhere?"
Oh, America – oh, *my* Turtle Island – this was never
how my people thought of "making it," paving our Mother
over with cocksure money-making buildings, concrete
hearts, with "How many people did you *fuck* today?"

No, you didn't admit it was your first time. Yes, I didn't say
how unsure I felt even though I'd been on this ride before.
The pinnacle we arrived at floated in an altered world.
I had gone all around the old one, but this was like
journeying home when all familiar faces have disappeared.
That evening when we edged out onto Empire State Building
observation deck, your face was the only face in the entire
universe that I knew. In those sky clouds swirling
in crashing mists, bloodied winds, you held me tight
against wall that kept us from falling into New York's infinite
grid of neon stars, your face the sole one I still had faith in.
They had to close half the deck that night of your first time
being so high in skyscraper-sway with me, your arms forming
an aerie for our eagle's laughter, "'Scuse us while we kiss the sky!"

"What is that?" You asked in your first-time voice,
pointed to two blue ethereal light beams flowing past clouds.
Our faces traced their paths down to where 9/11 dead
still roamed through Twin Tower ghosts. "It's from *there*" –
our voices became one with the red winds. Two lights
that some artist – some poet like you, like me – had decided
to shine into torn sky. Two paths to the Spirit World. And, yes,
it was the first time for millions of people in America, but not
for my Turtle Island people. Not for the first people of Manhattan
murdered by white Christian terrorists. I saw in my Earth-heart
all the Indian lovers who grabbed each other's hands, leapt into
the waters of sorrow surrounding their island, their hooped homeland
of great blue ethereal herons of light. My eyes heard their screams.

So you bowed your face to mine, and our skin that night
became a prayer of thousands of tiny wings together.
You didn't tell me it was your first time here.
I grabbed your hand tight. I pulled you inside.

YOUR AMERICA, MY TURTLE ISLAND

In your America, you watch CNN for hours,
eat junk food, cheer your cowboy-president
when he brags about invading Iraq.
In my Turtle Island, I watch polluted sky
through South Side window, imagine
what Binghamton was like before the white man
invaded these hills, this river valley.

In your America, your flags sprout
on your porches like dyed carnations –
red, white, blue in a forced spring.
In my Turtle Island, I grow flowers
in small pots filled with the earth
your America stole from us.

In your America, no one dies when you bomb
human beings in another country.
They just get liberated.
In my Turtle Island, I grow a red geranium
for my mother who died of *your* cancer,
a white gardenia for my father who died
for *your* freedom in your "Good War,"
a blue violet for the sky of my heart.

In your America, you make believe
that everyone lives in a nuclear family,
instead of the nuclear fission of dysfunction.
In my Turtle Island, I'm a mixed blood Indian woman
who loves a Korean-American poet
with a full blood's eyes and hair –
and a Persian cat, our daughter,
color of Iraqi sands.

In your America, you shout "Democracy,"
even though money is king, and brings
your God into it. The one I don't trust.
In my Turtle Island, I speak my vision with what
Haudenosaunee people call the Peacemaker's voice.
I only need enough fried bread to live on
and silence for the Great Mystery.

In your America, you support Homeland Security,
confident no soldier or policeman will ever force you
onto a Trail of Tears, no lawyer, no trial.
In my Turtle Island, people are too poor to buy
their way out of reservations, cockroach-slums,
jail archipelagos. I know what it's like
to be invaded by *your* freedom.

In your America,
will you ever know how it feels to love
a family, a tribe, this sweet bitter beautiful country,
my broken home —
the way I have loved
my Turtle Island for centuries?

WHIM (for Barbara Mann, who has helped me keep my true heart)

AIM, *sekoh*! Big, badass, butt-beautiful Native men
who look like you are posing for 19th century "End of the Trail"
Curtis photographs in washed out browns, here's my *hello*:
"You've arrived." Once ballsy bro's, your American Indian Movement
is dead. You stereotypes paralyzed in sepia, you who brag
about Government enrollment cards claiming you are
real American Injuns, I am galloping in with your eulogy
"in the spirit of Crazy Horse" – so sing your death song.
AIM, you claimed at Alcatraz sit-in and Wounded Knee uprising
that you had dreamed giving us back our pride, our dignity.
And I rode that dream bareback for many sweet moons
until I realized some of you were playing to the white man
who always ignored us Indian women when he wasn't raping us,
using us to cook his food, feed his ego. AIM, one of you
murdered Anna Mae Aquash when all those years you told us
Dreamer Women the FBI dumped Anna in a ditch to die.
AIM, too many of you are prancing around in Hollywood flicks,
bucks making big bucks, while the rest of us are made more
and more invisible by genocide. So, yeah, with any due respect
for what you did give to me, to us – you and traitorous sisters
who wave BIA cards like American *Amerigo Vesupucci* flags
that shut us out – AIM, our love affair is ash.

Heartbroken, un-enrolled Indian brothers and sisters, you
of mountain and woodlands freedom, you who have foxes
lay soft faces in your hands, fawns bow to you in wild fields,
blue birds alight on your voices opened up with trusting song,
I am exercising my own stereotype today, my woman's prerogative
in living color. I am treating myself to a woman's whim.
Dear brothers and sisters descended from ancestors who fought
fiercely for the far-in places of Mother Earth, for quietness,
for moss, ferns, rivers, pure air, sparklings of light, eagle hearts,
today I start WHIM, the *Woodlands Hotties Indian Movement*.
Today I who can claim no ties to any reservation, no chains,
no ancestors who got barbed wired inside a concentration camp,
no Government card for proof I'm indigenous, no FDA
APPROVED RED MEAT stamped across my proud Indian ass –

I invite you into a new movement, movement of round dance,
movement of Eastern Woodlands women who understand equality
between men and women, movement of people who live
their Indian love medicine every eternity of their lives
that despise clock-time and the time bomb of politically correct
Native Americans selling out to casinos, cards, cruelty.
On this day, I and my long haired sisters hot enough to burn up
anyone's attempt to tame us – today our smiling-eyed men
almost as hot as we are – today *all of us*, *Akwe:gon*, round dance
our fierce, tender, woodlands' freedom, our wake for AIM,
our awakening WHIM. Friends, we invite you in.
Akwe:gon. Akwe:gon.

SEXIEST TRIBE IN AMERICA

Hardly a day goes by that I don't meet a Cherokee man, woman, child.
I could write a book about how I meet them – at powwows, or
reading my Native Pride bumperstickers when I roll a grocery cart
to my Indian car, or through my poetry, a mutual friend, and even
on the street, dancing up to me, babbling, "Are you an Indian?" –
and when I say, "Yeah" – announcing they're from Cherokee Nation.
Then I usually add, "You know how Will Rogers, *Cherokee*, used to say
he never met a man he didn't like? As a woman I probably wouldn't
go *that* far, but I have never met a Cherokee I didn't like."
Whoever all these Cherokees are, such sentiment is almost so,
except for my one Cherokee friend's ex-wife who called me up,
yelled she found a rough draft of a letter her former man
wrote to me and if I told anybody about those ceremonies
and sacred fire and the boogers she would drive from Tennessee
to Binghamton, New York, then punch me in the face. I drawled
I never met a Cherokee I didn't like and pretty soon I had her purring
exactly like my cat while I perched admiring my green-eyed face
in the looking glass, flying around my poet's finger gleaming
with that opal ring her ex gave me. Yes, Cherokee people –
one Southerner used to call me *Sugar Puddin'*, pretended
he wasn't married when he asked me out to dinner. One chief
at a powwow had his men "take care of" a Yakima asshole
who made my sister and me cry by lording it over us with his
Government card, telling us our grandfather was stupid for not
staying on a reservation. One actor regaled me with stories
of being in Hollywood movies, sent me Leanin' Tree cards
while I had love medicine dreams about Bill Clinton, Elvis
and Jimmy Hendrix, yep, all Cherokee. And the letter writer
from the Great Smokies beaded me my medicine bag,
then died in a way that almost left me forever bitter –
except he made me promise to keep beading the light.
Once I was at a Woodstock reunion in Bethel. My sister and I
happily were talking to a childhood Sioux friend of ours, catching up
on our lives since twenty years ago, laughing about our days
as Indian playmates, friend telling us about his Cherokee ex-wife
and their intertribal warfare. I grinned, "Wow, you married
a Cherokee? There are so many of those around. They have to be

the sexiest tribe in America!" This man kneeling nearby rose up,
all seven feet of him, hair rivering over his shoulders like burnt
sweetgrass. In his warrior's voice he whooped, "Sexiest, huh?
Hey, I'm Cherokee." I could have rested my case right then and there.
Had I not been married, maybe I would have celebrated
the 25th anniversary of Woodstock Nation by fucking that Cherokee
that night right beneath his AIM flag by his soft fire under the same stars
our ancestors dreamed into. I even know a "mixed blood" who feels
he isn't enough Cherokee to claim it. How can I explain this makes him
sexier than all the rest of them? And given how it is with me, I wonder
if I'm a Cherokee princess when I howl in bed.

FEAR

Channel surfing, you stop at documentary
on dolphins. Sleek, they weave
through water, arc sparkling past
Hokusai waves into blue air. You flash
back to your former life of Florida winters,
sunning on Gulf's white sand, waiting
for dolphins to swim near.

You called them with your silence, they came,
you pretended they danced between water and sky
because you loved them enough to sing their language.

Then you can't watch anymore.

Film images burst past TV screen –
Japanese fisherman slaughtering dolphins
because they ruined the fishing. Hundreds
bleed into ocean, tides swirl pink,
carcasses heaped side by side,
flapping, heaving for breath.

You switch it off with black remote.

There is something here you need to say
because maybe if you say it
you will never feel you are a dying
dolphin again. No asthma, no
heart storming interior seas
like red tsunami.

It has to do with fear.

With being hurt from so far back
you bleed out into what should only
be beautiful – sea – river – lake,

beach on that shore you swore
you'd never return to.

What if you could love yourself enough
to learn your own language, dance
between earth and sky?

Or at least pretend to?

BEFORE CHRISTMAS THAT YEAR (for Danny)

Before Christmas that year, Danny and I sneaked into
our parents' bedroom. The Christmas gifts that Santa Claus
was bringing us were piled on the closet floor in shadow
and beneath my mother's medicine cabinet of whiskies.
We started quickly feeling the wrappings of poinsettias
and snowflakes, until my fingers brushed something and
the package in my hands lit up. The light beneath the paper
glowed, and I shook the gift ever so slightly. "Danny,
what do you think this is?," I asked, and he took the long
slender gift and shook it a little harder. But neither of us
could guess. We managed to push the bump and the light
disappeared, and we saw the light of the western sun also
slowly skate across the bedroom door. We heard our mother
walk down the stairs from where she had been sewing, and
we slipped out of the room she and our father slept in, that
mysterious room where their voices floated late into the nights.
And only on Christmas Eve did I see the package again,
the one we shook and hoped we didn't break. My fingers
fumbled with it, tearing off its gold sparkly ribbon and pulling
off scotch tape at the seams, until I drew out a long stick
at whose end was a silver star as sparkly as the ribbon.
And then I found the bump and I pushed it and the star
lit up, and my mother's and father's and Danny's faces
lit up, and the faces of my other brothers and my baby sister.
And now after all these years I can see their faces in the
dark of me, as once more our lives quietly steal into colder weather,
and sometimes still there is a small curious hand
in the forbidden shadows that accidentally lights up
hidden gifts.

CATSKILL (for Boonie)

Your mother asked you and the others
to promise she'd remain at home.
Don't take me back to the hospital. Let me
die in the Catskills where it's beautiful. And
you all promised. How she died that winter
you, your brothers, your sister
barely can speak of. Twenty years later
when people mention breast cancer
you stare far into each other's faces
to where extinct panthers scream in silence.

It got into her bone, and something else
got into your bones that bitter February.
Occasionally you and your sister talk about
the night your mother begged the two of you
to kill her. You suppose this is why even in summer
it is always snowing in you. One would think
you would never wish to return to a place
of such sorrow, to mountains you grew up in
but left early for the big cities
and other bohemians to be with.

The last winter you went back, you sat
in The Sit 'n Bull with a male cousin, also a poet.
After you both had drunk your fifth Thunderbird
while solving the mysteries of this universe, your cousin
burst out over "Crazy" hazing from jukebox,
Listen, listen, don't say anything for awhile.
Listen to the way these mountain people speak,
how soft it is, how musical, how like our rivers. So you
sat there and he held your sad hand red from window neon.
Someday you would make him promise.

TWEED (for Shine Eyes)

If I had ever seen you in that tweed coat before, I had forgotten it
between last winter and this. But you came breezing in through
the door almost like a man I had never met, in a coat
I would have imagined on a male fashion model, not on you
so given to wearing muted grays and beige. But this coat
was what I sometimes yearned to slip around your shoulders,
a classy version, say, of Joseph's coat of many colors. So today
I sat across from you for close to an hour after you smoothed the coat
across an empty chair, and we talked about Indians and Jews and
how we have been treated in the same genocidal ways and about
everything except that coat listening in the corner. I wondered if it
heard me think how I would like to accessorize it with eagle feathers,
beaded moccasins, and a medicine bundle with the wolves
of my clan protecting you. I finally got around to it, just as I
was about to leave. I finally said, "What a beautiful tweed coat.
Where did you get that from? Look at those reds, so subtle, rivering
through its thicknesses of blacks and whites." You warned me
my question was going to bring an answer beyond what even I might
imagine. You said, "Oh, the coat belonged to my brother. And that
is what he was like – gay, but subtle about it, with good taste." I floated
my hand across the tweed, the red like blood, not quite touching it.
And the red made me think of your brother who died of AIDS
at the very beginning, before we foresaw anything like an HIV-plague
or yesterday's World Aids Day. And, Jesus, you were so handsome
dashing in out of the November day in that tweed with blood tint
all through it, in that coat of a brother whose blood got tainted
in some lost, happy act of young man lovemaking. I don't know
why you wear this coat. Maybe for the same reason I sleep at night
beneath the brown shawl that I bought for my mother in Sligo,
the one with subtle yellows glowing through it. She died
with that shawl wrapped around what was left of her, even her bones
gnawed by cancer to nothing. At first, I wasn't sure I would keep it.
Cancer stench clung to its wool and I had it dry-cleaned twice
after the funeral, cried over my mother rotting while still alive.
But now I fall asleep wrapped in her shawl and her dreams
of flying to Ireland and finding her castle next door in England
and, in a long tweed coat, wandering around on a windy moor the way

her ancestors did before they sailed here and made love with Indians
whose eyes looked like haunted heaths, whose blood most whites
considered tainted. Maybe when your brother wore that rich
tweed coat he was royalty in his castle. Maybe when you wear it,
you are king in a land more shining than this one, land where a brother
comes back alive and smiling. It is something like that with me
and my mother when I sleep beneath fringed shawl her ashes
dream springtime yellow in.

SHADOW DREAM (for Libby)

You were walking in a dream that had no weather.
In a body that cast no shadow you were wandering
down a sidewalk that had no city. You were drifting
in a place of no day, no night. Oh, beautiful dreamer woman,
you wandered through all the ages of yourself, blue-eyed
infant, girl, maiden, teacher, lover, mother, spinner
of spells. You were stumbling down a trail of laughter
that smelled of tears. You were staggering in a dream
woven from the wonderment of men who couldn't
forget your head's proud tilt, the way you shook gold
hair across their sleeping hearts until they woke
to fairy tales, again. You were a Cherokee princess
walking west. You were the good witch who couldn't
help being so bewitching that men metamorphosed
into red wolves when you flamed by.

You were straying in a dream whose eyes were silent howls.
"Elizabeth! Elizabeth!" You whirled around. A mouthless
woman, hat crushed to grey/blonde hair, was limping
in your dream. She hunched beneath moth-eaten coat,
legs coffined inside seamed nylons, feet trapped in broken
shoes. Shadow hunting for its body, she hobbled
towards you. Paralyzed, you stood inside all the beautiful ghosts
of yourself. "Elizabeth!" Like a Dorothea Lange photograph
of black-and-white hunger, the grey-faced stranger
embraced you. You tried to speak, scream, "Let me go!"
You moved your tongue in a dream which had no mouth.
Crone in torn wool coat clutched you closer, crushed
your breasts into petals of dormant pain. You were
floundering in a dream that had no moon, no sun.
You were breathless in a dream that had no waking.
You knew you had breast cancer. You knew the crone
in Great Depression coat was your future lurching
to greet you. Oh, beautiful dreamer woman —
Cherokee sister — red wolves howl
at your flaming by.

WINTER'S END WHITE DREAM

You trudge through mountain snow – legs aching, pulling
against it. You are close to falling, the way you feel
in waking life. There is small light in the air, as if the sun's rays
collapsed down into snow crystals, months of white
patterned into vast drifts. The air smells faintly of hemlock –
faintly of nothing. You are alone. You don't even see
a starving deer, a startled rabbit. No birds appear.
The trail you made opens out into a lopsided clearing –
and a white carousel tilted towards frozen pond.
The carousel looks carved from ice. You walk over to it,
legs creating deep holes as you go.
You swing your legs over the first animal of the carousel,
sit there, face to the cold. The carousel moves.
You glance down. What you thought was a wood animal,
a painted pony, is not that at all. Your legs straddle
a swan. Delicate. White. Strong. You bow your face to
swan face. One green eye stares up at you like an emerald.
The carousel picks up speed, you and swan flying
in circles of white movement. As you fly you hear feathers
of calliope music, the whistling of birds, the song
of the third-eyed swan. In between – silence.
White.
In your own green eyes lie the leafless trees past
the carousel, the pond, the snow. Above the forest
shines swan-colored sky. Your hair lifts up
like wings. Silver. Your mouth drinks the dream
of spring. Gold. And you can't get over the beauty
of one eye gazing so softly, *greenly*, up at you.

RIDING WITH GOLD

RIDE WITH THE GOLD, mixed-blood Indian woman
reads gold commandment on back of bus polluting
Parkway ahead of her. Beneath its looming words
Sacagawea and her mixed-blood baby gaze sideways
from a moon-size coin. *Liberty*, it glitters. *In God we trust*.
The woman flashes her high beam on Sacagawea's face, face
family members say remind them of *her* in her younger days.
The face burns ghost-like gold through November night lit
not by stars but street lights, car lights, lights for Parkway Liquor,
Holiday Inn, Video King, golden-arched McDonald's — electric
seductions for those riding with the gold. The woman
sways with vertigo, suddenly lost on this Parkway clone
to countless suburban strips and hungry nights across America
she's wandered down. A boy grinning through rear bus window
flips her the finger, feather-like, above Sacagawea's head.
Mixed-blood woman shoots him the bird, switches back
to low beam. "Oh, Sacagawea," she whispers, "did you know
it would get as lonely as this? Did you dream when you led
Lewis and Clark through sweet-smelling forest, wildflower fields,
it would end like this? When you had your mixed-blood child
by your French 'squaw-man', did you feel in the agony of birth
it would lead to mixed-breed pain like this? Oh, beautiful Shoshone
Bird Woman, when you died of White Man's disease at twenty-five,
did you realize how much our wings were about to be torn?"
The woman's eyes tear at Parkway lights, storm clouds
of bus exhaust. She sees in first snow flurries
people who horde Sacagawea coins in cookie tins and jelly jars.
"They're gonna be worth something someday," they lecture her.
She's too exhausted to disillusion them with one of their clichés —
"All that glitters is not gold." She's too tarnished in her own heart
to shout that the shiny dollar of a face they're collecting
once possessed a shining heart. Mixed-blood Indian woman
drives down asphalt edges of her life lit by fake lights.
Sacagawea's face floats close to words used to kill off
the Indian. *Liberty*. *God*. *Trust*.

DRIVING HOME TONIGHT

Driving home tonight from the Angela Davis lecture,
I wanted to forget all she said about prisons
and backdoor slavery and how many more
minorities are in prison than whites. Driving home
the lights across the Susquehanna twinkled
like the stars of my mountain childhood –
the road curved like a dream along the curve
of the hill, as it became a trail of taillights,
headlights, and memories shining far back
to Catskills, where I used to be cradled in
my mother's arms as my father drove Old Route 17
at night between Liberty and Livingston Manor.
The car lights were like stars come down to earth,
and it seemed all I had to do was reach out the old
Chevy window to gather them in my small hands.
Now my hands grow wrinkled, my eyes
weighed down with 53 years of highways
and the truckstops of knowledge. I thought of you
as I drove by the river, of the time you were
in jail and of the white man who put you there.
He's dead now and all this beauty of road and water
will never be his. You are alive, great heron
blazing up blue as night memory,
free as love.

BERING STRAIT BINARY STAR

I.

I am the woman who walked away from the campfire.
I am the woman who strode out into snow.
I am the woman who left her tribe's familiar faces.
I am the woman who wanted to see the stars better.
I am the woman who wandered until she could no longer see the old fire.
I am the woman who trudged so far only the stars were her fire.
I am the woman who sank deep in snow glinting in star-light.
I am the woman of high cheekbones, Asian eyes.
I am the woman whose eyes searched for a constellation
to guide her back. I am the wild woman
who missed her husband out in the snow.
I am the woman who started to freeze beneath stars that flamed no heat.
I am the woman who started to weep for her man.
I am the woman who began to wail for her man's eyes,
deepnesses of earth inside river curves.
I am the woman who fell to that earth beneath the snow.
I am the woman who dug to touch the earth
the way she touched her man's flesh.
I am the woman on all fours who tried to find her mate's fingers
reaching for hers as she floundered in snow.
I am the woman who stood back up.
I am the woman whose tears froze on her fire-less face for centuries.
I am the woman who walked on in silence.
I am the lost woman who followed a binary star.
I am the woman who stumbled across the Bering Strait.
I am the woman who started new tribes in a strange land.
I am the woman who waited in snow at the beginning of centuries
of hunger, disease, hatred, self-hatred, genocide.
I am the woman who never forgot her husband dreaming
into the campfire.

II.

You are the husband who stayed by the campfire
cradling the son and daughter you had with the woman.
You are the man who sang to the woman, your fur-clothed children.
You are the man who told stories to the tribe.
You are the man who wove magic with rhyme.
You are the man whose fingers touched the woman's skin
into chant, pictographs, dance, song.
You are the man with the faint yellow of tundra-sun in his skin.
You are the shaman who crouched by the fire, woke
from his dreaming.
You are the man whose heart wandered out after the woman.
You are the man who wailed for his woman's eyes,
green of earth in short summers.
You are the man who cried for the story skin of his wife's body.
You are the man who hunted for centuries for his lost wife.
You are the man left behind when the land bridge was broken.
You are the husband whose heart broke like March ice.

I am the woman who found her husband after centuries of crying.
You are the man who found his wife after centuries of tracking
the binary star of my silence.

THE LAST WORDS (for Johnny)

> *"Imagine if you were the last person on earth to know English.*
> *Imagine how you would feel about that." John Smelcer*

You come to my country, Iroquois country, from Alaska.
I get to speak to you, the invited poet, at Lost Dog Café –
dinner you don't know I invited myself to. I wonder
why the professors let me crash this gathering for another
Indian. I pretend they fear I'll toss my tomahawk at them
for the way they've treated me and other Indians here.

So I smile over Greek chicken while you tell the women
from the English Department how badly you've been treated
up there, in Alaska. "Awful," they ooze, and I figure
they might like to get laid by you. Meanwhile, I no longer
can pay for health insurance and wonder if I'll like
making love in a cardboard box on State Street.

We talk about blood quantum, boarding schools
other genocidal things they did to us. We speak
of our high suicide rate, how your brother killed himself
when he was 23. You say you have wanted to do
the same. I know that desire. I am laughing,
underneath remembering I nearly died at 13.

Later, at the reading, you speak of your Native tongue,
read poems you wrote in Ahtna. After the elders all die
you will be the last to know this language that now bears me
back to Catskills I grew up in, its deep mountains, the foxes
who come to me and the exterminated panthers. Rivers
I could fly my body into so I might float to a quiet sea.

And far inside me I weep for all men like you, with that color
in your eyes, blue forest shadow, your hearts deep
as the mountains I am always homesick for. When it is over
I buy your book with its cover the color of the skin we Indians
are supposed to have. You sign it to me in Ahtna – "Kazuun,"
"Beautiful." Then I drive snowy roads to my apartment whose rent

soon I won't be able to pay. I whisper your "Beautiful" aloud, for
I read once that sound soars out to space forever. Maybe it wings
in, as well. I sing "Kazuun" like a prayer. Perhaps this will be the last
word of your language. Word that made a woman feel beautiful enough
not to commit suicide. Word that made millions of icy stars
glisten inside winter sky of her.

WHITE DRESS

What if she had gotten married in a white dress?
Done the whole thing with white Victorian house
circled by white picket fence surrounded by white
cowboy capitalists who hated *red* and *scarlet*?

What if she had never *felt free*, traveled cross-country,
had an utter incapacity to love bankers and lawyers,
missed being called *squaw*, *bitch*, *witch*, *cunt*, *crazy hippie*?
What if she had gotten married in a white dress?

What if she had been born with none of that
Red Indian blood further crimsoned by femaleness?
What if she had never been fearless despite her fear?
What if her *scarlet lady* had never felt free to love freely?

What if she had lived her green-eyed life circled by white
picket fence instead of stars and fairies, mesas and ravens?
What if she had never opened her thighs to blue starlight? If
in a parallel universe Coyote hadn't taught her wild rose ecstasy?

What if she could yet grow respectable, un-talked about,
moneyed and matronly? What if she never wrote another poem,
sang for beauty, risked safety for love? What if she bought the white
dress? What if she did the whole colorless thing before she died?

RAVEN GOES TO COLLEGE

After many years Raven decided to get his doctorate. His bright
eyes noticed a lot of birds and Indians acquired English accents
when they studied Brit Lit, except when they "talked" theory.
Then their noses pinched shut until they sounded French. This
music of mated pomposity tickled Raven, made him feel
he was licking the sun wobbling between his beak again.

Raven's Shakespeare professor lectured how *really*
the men in Will's plays were women, the women
men. Raven suspected his female professor was *really*
a man. He was getting bored with this shit, but muted
his gregarious self so he'd get an "A". Raven slouched
blackly in his chair manufactured by prisoners.

It snowed. Raven squawked, "Fuck it,"
decided to fly from Northwest to Northeast Woodlands.
He had met a Mohawk woman at a powwow, theorized
her shiny smile and eyes might teach him more than college.
Raven flapped and flew towards October fire, the twinkling
stars, moon and sun helping him on his way.

PASSING

("*The trouble with Normal is
it always gets worse.*" Bruce Cockburn)

On a cold November night like this, I think about passing.
I always imagined I could do that on the surface, on my body —
do things like have my hair cut by the best gay hairdresser in town,
permed, then dyed a discrete blonde. And I could start wearing
a brassiere, a white one, and girdles, stockings, and beige blouses,
short skirts and low-heeled pumps. And I would cease wearing
beaded earrings in my ears. I would only wear pearls quiet
as the bottom of the sea. Because on a cold November night
I am tired of being Indian, wonder if life would be easier
if I didn't look different, if I could disguise the Indian-ness,
could hide that old happy wildness that has to do with
truth-speaking and dancing dreams and praying in deep forests.
Once I mentioned this to an elder, swore I would dress up
as Normal for Halloween. He chuckled that even if I wore
my pinstriped suit, straight-pinned my hair into a bun,
something would still shine through, some strand
of silver hair shoot loose, vision break open
into New Mexico sky, heart flame quicken my walk
into fancy dance. But it's been one of those days that only
Indian people can know, kind where we find out someone
who claims to be one of us — *isn't.* One of those days
when someone who always spoke about honoring people —
dishonored the honorable ones. One of those days when I end
wondering what happened to us, even though I know too well
what happened to us and wish I could forget it, wish I were
a Catskill child still trailing after my Indian grandfather
and pet raccoon who seemed to live on his left shoulder,
wish the view out my window were mountains, not
city lights. But there are no stars here to wish on, unless
I can count those glow-in-the-dark stars on garret ceiling,
ones the drug dealer stuck there before I rented the place.
On a cold November night like this things feel so confused,
so lonely, I almost yearn to be in one of those sweats non-Indians
go to, then question why I have never been to one. And being
a real Indian, I am too polite to say, "Because you're there

and all the sweats in the Milky Way wouldn't purify you."
Yes, possessing the "blood" can make me savage sometimes.
But maybe if I could take *that* and the mix of it, I could
homogenize with the white part of me, not care anymore
about how we got in this fix, one where "I was Indian
before being Indian was cool" but keep meeting others
who waited until being Indian was safe, exotically normal,
like belonging to the most beautiful family that ever was.
On this November night long as my hair, I am smiling
because even they got our beauty right.

WHEN I AM A TREE

When I am a tree it is always October, my birth month.
And it is Catskills, where I was born and grew up.
When I am a tree, I am all blaze in the arms of my branches,
garnet and gold. When I am a tree I am filled with eagles,
the sky is one of those autumn blues, no clouds
the hue of winter. When I am a tree
and the roots of me feel a sky-eyed Indian man
walking fox-like on earth, making the sap of me
tremble delicately at his approach, I am all leaves,
all rustle in breeze, all song waiting to be hugged
when I am a tree.

I WISH I HAD WRITTEN THIS POETRY

Whenever the train slows through another southern town
your face flashes — back alley lights flickering across dark
window your face is doubled in. Night glimpses of
diapers, work pants, K-Mart dresses — on the other side
of the tracks the raiments of life hung by women's hands
from sagging clotheslines, shining like this in passing
eyes. The women are sleeping, the empty streets
radiating out like lines in a dreaming face. Your face flashes,
darkens, in window. We leave behind another small town.
You turn to me, take my hand in yours as if my unread palm lines
were empty streets that needed filling. In this Amtrak sleeper
with its rock-and-rhythm of all the lovers' bodies of all the nights
in the world, you recite poetry to me from Persian poet, Rumi,
traveling seven centuries back. *Don't go anywhere without me.*
Let nothing happen in the sky apart from me, or on the ground —
What made that bliss-drunk poet hop a Florida-bound train
in this American February? I have come so far, seeing your face
turned towards me, Rumi's poetry in the soft movements
of your mouth, kiss whirling in my ear. I have come so far
from the small northern town I grew up in, hearing
the Ontario & Western's slow roar at town's edge
in the wreck of night, in my young eyes the raiments of life
left by sleeping women. When would my Beloved come,
carry me away on a south-bound train? When would we leave
town after dreaming town behind, at sunrise wake to a country
of flowers? The Beloved's face turned towards me. "I wish
I had written this poetry for you," you say.
I say, "You have."

THE DIRT IN THE GALLERY ACROSS FROM
THE OLD WHOREHOUSE ON STATE STREET

This winter seems a dream imploded into nightmare. You tell yourself
it is ridiculous to hate the weather, yet you hate this day-after-day
of mercury bleeding below the zeros of a half-million thermometers.
And snow, *more snow*. And trees a calligraphy of despair smudging
hills beyond city rooftops. You hate the trees and nor'easters
and how the birds have ceased singing. One Saturday when the sun
reveals itself, you visit art galleries. You wander into John Ros'
State Street gallery, second floor past steps like those in a recurring
dream you have. You encountered John in Barnes & Noble once.
You figure if you don't like what he does you can always just admire
him. That would go along with the general dream-tone of 2004
war-time winter – ice-haired Native poet practicing art appreciation
of young American artist who pulls off looking like Lord Byron
in Binghamton, NY, home of the Twilight Zone. The trees don't
approach his smolder. You glide onto hardwood floor, light slashing
through old building's tall windows, wood gleaming. John stands
by far wall, looking symbolic. A huge rectangle of dirt
inhabits the room's center, like dirt piled up after another Indian
gets buried. On top of the dirt three clear plastic rectangles, no
sacred hoops here. You are ravenous for dirt. What Indian woman
can bear being separated from earth for as long as you've been
separated? You kneel, press your naked hands to it. And it
feels so warm and good after feeling only snow for centuries.
"Have you considered planting flower seeds in this?" you ask John.
He gives you his sensitive-haughty Lord Byron smile. The ghosts
in the old whorehouse across the street spread their legs.
You will return, drop some blue morning glory seeds
into the dirt.

BEAR

At first she didn't know what to do
when she was walking in summer light
towards Willowemoc,
glanced down,

couldn't think
what it could be, brain
synapses stopped, brief
infinity, *Oh*

Bear.

Nor did she even know who she was,
some girl sauntering in summer light
towards Catskill river.

Some Indian girl who had a bear
swaying close to her thighs, not just
any bear but a small happy brown bear,
a half-grown bear, glancing
back up at her,

inviting her to float her
hot glowing summer's hand to bear dance,
stroke fur from earth brown to fire.

So there they were,
Bear and Indian girl
sauntering towards a river
with an Indian name whose meaning
had been lost so long ago
no one remembered
when the meaning died.

There she was, hearing Grandfather tell her,
Never touch wild animals. Never disrespect

their world by luring them into human tameness,
craziness, through touch, through leaving scent,
through any human words or thought.

Oh Bear, Oh Bear.

Hard not to stroke such shining
from bear country, *the fur, the fur, the eyes,*
eyes inviting her, Indian girl

journeying with Bear to river
with name that some humans
touched too close once,
strangers forcing Indian girls
into a tamer world.

Nor did she even know who she was.

They walked for a long time towards the river,
she never reached it, she floated on
into the other side of dream,
she was waking up in one more city
empty of bears.

She knew who she was.
She cried.

WHALE WATCH (for Ronny Guijs)

She had never seen one. She grew up
in Catskills, swam along river bottoms
with rainbow trout. Whenever she drifted
towards sleep, heard highway trucks blaze
darkly east, she hungered to hitchhike
to the Great Salt Lake as ancestors called it.
Sleeping, she dreamed of whales.
Some nights, when Whale surfaced
like a great grey hill, she leapt onto
his back that plunged her glistening in
and out of sea, down to corals, anemones,
clawed and colored strangenesses
her tongue had no names for.

This is why she swayed now at fast moving
boat prow, hair whipping silver across face
until it shed her many masks. Sister yelled,
"Pinch your skin, feel how sticky, how slimy!"
They were on a whale watch beyond
Boothbay, Maine, July day graying until air
appeared as ethereal, mythical whale. The captain
drove them way out – but no whales, just
mirrored shadows of small Jesus birds skimming
the braiding waves. Sister urged her, "Lean forward,
spread your arms like wings," so she lifted her arms,
singing, "I am queen of the world, I am queen
of the world," drinking the salt wind.

Still no whales. Back to pinching arms, cheeks.
Flesh like fish, flashing scales. "We may be
changing to fish or mermaids," she laughed
to sparkling sister at moment she spotted
not a humpback but some creature more unusual –
Not your typical American football-for-brains-male.
Materialized at runaway infinity where she spoke
the word metamorphosis, when he didn't know she
secretly smiled after she asked, "Would you like me to

take a picture of you with your camera," and he said "No"
as though he believed with the old ones his spirit might be
stolen. "Oh, and how will you know you were on this boat?"
Creature circled elegant fin-fingers near hair
alchemizing to seaweeds golden-brown, shone
"I'll keep it all in here."

Maybe had it not been for Bailey's Irish Cream Firewater
she and sister swilled down to warm cold winds out of them,
maybe then she and that tallness of male human
with Sky Spirit eyes, sea-combed hair, Indian red shirt,
never would have spoken a second time. But she was riding
a blaze of tipsiness like wild horses, and there was
something of the proud unbridled chief about him.
Maybe it was because the captain announced the whales
were endangered while the boat raced like her heart
feeling sorrowful because she knew she, too,
was endangered.

Or perhaps it was some sadness in this other one
who could be of Turtle Island but never of fast food America
fake in concrete. So this poem beaded like long ago days
of when traditional people first met, held their hearts open
as if inside tender blossomed hands, sacred drums of them
drawing seeming strangers into a dance of metamorphosis,
perceiving *that* of elusive whale in each other.
So thank you, new friend from Netherlands,
for how you spoke to this Turtle Island woman,
for words of knowledge and wise understanding
regarding my people and the stolen land
I am forever homesick for.

My brother, Nya:weh.

PEMAQUID (for Pogie)

Older brother drives you and sister
to Pemaquid Point. Not knowing
if you will return to Maine
you kneel on great granite boulders
jutted up from Atlantic low tide,
fingers searching for whatever sparkles
like that day's waves — mica, gneiss,
feldspar, quartz — slipping glintings
into bag flowered open
off sunlit shoulder.

Back in New York you wash sand from
stone, study such shinings inside hands'
paling sunburn. Like all your family
you revel in rocks, wild to collect them
despite recollections of bad jokes —
wives, husbands, friends teasing,
"You have rocks in your heads.
Why lug home more earth chunks,
festoon rooms with fossils, minerals, stone?"

How sparkling *you* are, cradling each heft
of Earth, layered stories that won't be trapped
in mere words. How *radiant* on those shores
that lightnings of feldspar, black silvers of mica,
stars of quartz wash you to. That day
at Pemaquid — in its harbor of Indian ghosts,
glaciers long gone, earth scraped down
to the bones of centuries, you were three
"part Indian" kids again, as if a half
century hadn't come, then fled.

Yes, you always gathered stones that lack tongues,
won't speak of love in the usual ways.

HOLOCAUST MUSEUM

Now that they've torn down the wall in Berlin, Germany,
they're building a Holocaust Museum. Some say
it's backed by a secret benefactor — maybe
Crazy Horse, Oglala Sioux holy man
leaping off all those malt liquor bottles
that steal his name to destroy his people
and the sons and daughters of the poor.
Now that the wall is rubble, they're raising
a museum designed by the artist, Hundertwasser,
half-breed Jew who sees in circles like an Indian,
rooms rippling out in empty spaces where the wall was.
Each round room will bear witness to the Great Death,
genocide, cultural destruction of the native peoples
of the Americas. There has never been a museum
like it. What better place to put it
than in Berlin, Germany?

Now that the rubble has been sold as souvenirs,
step right up for the Holocaust Museum's grand opening.
That wild half-breed, Hundertwasser, outshone himself
this time, making the door canoe-shaped, fashioning rooms
like a turtle's back, a skin drum, tipi, a painted Peruvian
whistle, a broken bowl. Once inside the door each German
is handed a stone, beneath which the name and fate of one
human being trapped in the Holocaust will be revealed
at tour's end. One meaningful one among the mute millions.

The Germans file through, shaking their cultured heads
to the classical sounds of peyote music. It all seems
a nightmare hallucination — Columbus' sailors slicing small
children in half to test their sword blades, Kit Carson's
"Long Knives" cutting off women's breasts to use as balls
in barroom games, Turtle Island tribes left homeless
on their own lands. "How could human beings
do these things against other human beings?"

Past the rooms of soldier crimes, anthropologist
crimes, missionary crimes, the civilized German museum-goers
search for the answer in the room shaped like a horse's ass,
exposing the learned cracks of professors upon the subject
of red savages: "The Aztecs made human sacrifices, that's why
it was *de rigeur à la apropos* to do what we did for five
centuries." In the Holocaust Museum's last room shaped
like a child's tear, the appalled Germans read the United States
Government has never issued an apology to the people *it* slaughtered,
or drove into the heart's exile, and still do, unlike their Government
that finally apologized to the Jews. It is good to think
how terrible other people are. In the final tear-shaped room
the museum-goers flip over their stones in Berlin, Germany,
find nothing but stone there.

VINCENT VAN GOGH WRITES TO
JEANNE LOUISE CALMENT FROM THE STARS

"Artists are the Indians of the White Man's world." Lame Deer

Dear Madame Calment, now that you have lived to be 121, darling
of French intelligentsia along with Jerry Lewis and Derrida,
it is time I write to you from the whirling stars
as once I penned my heart's fire to Theo in those days of flame
when you, and others like you, snubbed me on the streets of Arles.
Oh, you were beautiful, Madame, the way only a 19th-century,
bourgeois girl could be, egg-washed hair twisted high
into a proud bun, torso corseted tight under a white dress,
eyes gleaming with dreams of a husband who would always provide
maids to iron your dresses flat and help keep your nose
at a haughty tilt. And, now, that fleeting beauty
of your scrubbed flesh fled, beauty I never desired
to brush on canvas, white on white, you brag to journalists
how you met me, a ragged artist, in your future in-laws' fabric shop.

You were thirteen and I, you gloat, was "ugly, disagreeable, sick."
I remember that day, Madame, the delicate cringe of your face
receding into the store's silken shadows when someone tried
to introduce us and you refused to speak, how I swallowed
the "Bonjour" risen in my throat back into God's silence.
Now that you are famous by the mere fact of having lived longer
than anyone else on earth, the journalists ask you, "But did you not hear
Vincent's voice?", moan when you say, "Mais, non," and demand
your Swiss chocolates and a glass of port.

Dear Madame Calment, the day I rushed blushing from that shop
with its piled fabrics meant to be sewn into clothing to conceal
human shame, I left you with your back turned in your virginal dress
and wandered out into the sunflowers, in among the stiff stalks
lifting soft petals up to Heaven. My heart filled with yellow,
my body sang in the heat with the whirring bees, the brush
in my trembling hand blazed into flame and burned my canvas
into flowers and fire that no one would buy. And, now, Madame,

you refuse to have your cataracts removed, cackle to your admirers
it's normal for ladies your age to be blind. But I knew
that day in the shop it was normal then for you. And even
with this obscene spinning of fortune's wheel in which the respectable
rich invest millions in my sunflowers, stars, and wife-less bed,
I know they're blind, too.

Dear Madame Calment, that night after I wandered
into the sunflower fields, I trudged back to Arles
bursting with love and starlight, yet seeing heavy-winged crows
flapping black across the dark places between stars. That night
I drifted towards the red lamps of the bordello, climbing
the steep steps behind my favorite whore, the straps
of her camisole slipping off her perfumed shoulders, her hair
streaming like Heraclitus' river across the dance and sway
of her plump hips. And there in bed, Madame, I entered
into the only kind of woman who would have me, entering her
the way I entered my canvases, until I became the body
of Christ and she my Magdalene, and all God's universe whirled
and sang in our bodies, our bodies in it, and I cried out to her,
"Dearly Beloved!"

Dear Madame Calment, it is time I write to you from the spiraling stars,
sorry that no man filled with the fire of flowers
ever sent you a piece of his ear, a shard of his beautiful madness.
When the journalists ask you how you've managed to live so long,
you joke, "I think God must have forgotten me."
Madame, maybe She has.*

* Madame has since been remembered

YELLOW GIRL, I GIVE YOU

You whose name I don't know, will never know,
you who danced in yellow ribbon dress edged in night blue,
you who helped call the sun back when you danced the round dance,
the woman's dance, the duck dance, the smoke dance,
I need to give you something after this fierce dog day
at Onondaga Nation, *your* nation. For when I watched you,
girl of bare brown legs, even browner moccasins,
you made me think of myself when I was ten and whirling
towards first womanhood. I saw how proud you were, how glad,
in the yellow dress I imagined your mother sewed for you, the way
my mother once sewed dresses filled with light for me.

Ondondaga girl of the soft smile, face raised to sky,
feet that caressed Mother Earth and flashed dreams in air,
I smiled each time I glimpsed your dance paintings. I remembered
when I was a girl and could dance my yellow across a rainy day
until the sun returned, as it did today after two downpours
and wildflower thunder. Yellow – always my favorite color, so
I followed you in your buttercup dress, the streams of its ribbons,
body and heart in synchronicity with the men's singing.
Yellow girl, *my* favorite dancer, you made me forget
the mud, the haze, the day's heat, the sweat that ribboned
my body. You reminded me *my heart is a sacred drum.*

Girl in yellow, whose name must be that of a beautiful bird,
when they had the dance contest I thought that you would win
first prize. Your hands were delicate wings floating through air,
your movements dignified as hope. But when the clanmother
announced who got third, second, and first prize, you got none.
You tried to keep your head high while you dragged back
to the hay bale that served as your chair, slumped down,
no longer smiled. And I remembered all the competitions
and smile-thefts from the time I was a child, asked myself
can this be Iroquois tradition – contests where children dance
for the white man's dollars?

So girl whose name I'll never know, when I noticed your tears
as I left the dance circle and hemlock arbor, your mother whispering
to you, I knew in my heart that felt like the day's rain breaking
across my eyes that I would do something to make it all up to you,
to me, to anyone who has ever been poor, who ever gave the earth
her dance, who ever believed in beauty or that life is fair. Yellow girl,
I give you no hundred dollars but my own humble offering
of a first prize, blue as a dress ribbon, this penniless poem.

FEAR OF BAG LADIES
(for Sigmund Freud, *in memoriam*)

The women you know have no fear of flying. They fly in airplanes
at the drop of a pin, a hat, a key – a thousand lovers easy
levitating with them between their thighs nine thousand feet up.
All around the world planes are penetrating sky. Women are having
Freud served to them as breakfast fruit. When it's over they stare down
at the upside-down underbellies of cloudscapes. The plane wings' long
shadows flow across petrified forests of orgasms – divine
phallic symbols, my dears, in between white ice-mountains glinting
suns back like compound eyes. In the old days the women you know
would have lit up. They have no fear of flying. When you ask them
how many flights they've taken, what the flight names were, they laugh
and can't recall – they've been on so many. But ask your friends
about bag ladies! Their faces snap together like puzzle pieces,
jigsaws of fear where bag ladies drag across their eyes, pupils,
dilated black mirrors of "There but for the grace of God go I."
The women you know have Master's Degrees, Ph.D.s. Some wear
diamond studs in their ears, some color their hair. Others paint visions
in oil, dream poems on the petrified forest of the frozen page.
It doesn't matter how smart they are, how beautiful they are,
how many men offer to take them for a ride on an airplane –
they're all convinced they could be bag ladies someday.

You consider Binghamton bag ladies, New York State cast-offs
stuck in Rod Serling's Twilight Zone where you live. Who couldn't be
the old woman with spiked white hair, purple coat draping down
to men's shoes, even in summer? Who couldn't age into that defiant
crone pulling a child's red wagon piled with unseen *who knows what*
inside Glad trash bags, parading sockless up and down Main Street,
singing "Wild Thing, you make my heart sing"? Business women rush
by her, hearing it, again, back in their safe houses – ringing their brains,
circling their square rooms – "Wild Thing"! Who couldn't be
the Cat Lady or the Bird Lady, devout bus-riders? In your hungry
student days of riding Broome County Transit, sometimes you shared
seats with the Cat Lady sporting her Five-and-Dime diadem,
its fake jewels – Queen for a Day, meowing, hissing, purring

at the speed of light. Nights, headed home, you'd nod off
to the Bird Lady chirping, trilling nearby, pigeon feathers plucked
from gutters poked in her canary-yellow hair, male bus driver grousing,
"I wonder what would happen if the Bird Lady met up with the Cat
Lady? Do ya think the Cat Lady would eat her?"

Yes, the women you know have no fear of flying. Yet all have a terror
of turning into ladies who believe they're cats, or birds, or immortal
girls bearing invisible possessions in Glad bags on red wagons shining
in sun, snow, rain – who sing "Wild Thing" until they drop off to sleep
at night next to a church wall. You listen for clues from your friends,
why they might become bag ladies, too – split mosaics of words
attempting to make sense of themselves in between everyday
polysyllabic jargon and wit. You hear, wedged inside laughter, slips
about growing up poor, being raped, being battered, being silenced,
being shamed, having secret nervous breakdowns made more secret
by Valium and Prozac. Maybe that explains it. Or maybe it's because
98% of the atoms in their bodies were not there a year ago.
Any morning they could wake up and – just like that! –
peek into mirrors and find bag ladies staring back at them. You try
to comfort the women you know who prefer airplanes to life on earth.
You quote Henry Miller to them, "I have no money, no resources,
no hope. I am the happiest man on earth." But your beautiful,
brilliant friends crow, "Oh, he's a man," ask that first question
every girl learns, "What do men know?" You stare down
at your unbuckled purple shoes. Your friends keep telling you,
"For Heaven's sake, buckle up. For Heaven's sake, you might
end up purring like a cat, trilling like a bird, singing
'Wild Thing' all day long!"

CANVAS (for Ruth Stone)

She decided to paint again after a quarter century,
set wood easel on table near north window, canvas
on that. The tubes of acrylic paint called her hands
to bright yellow. She had a story to tell,
one crying for yellow background. Half
the night she brushed yellow across white
until there was no white left. Her cat brushed
against her hot legs, after awhile
all she could feel was yellow, all
she could taste. She was getting
drunk on it, lay on the floor
to sleep it off.

Dawn. Still yellow. No
Galliano dream. She brewed tea,
lifted the brush for the story part. Spring
light darted across yellow, shadows
of leaves shook across lights. Her mouth
blossomed with smiles, the girl of her
loved yellow best. She stood there
growing old, brush poised in hand.
Crow's wing. Cloud across eyes.

She lay the brush down.

Yellow.

WHEN MY OLDEST BROTHER TURNS (for Hoppy)

When my oldest brother turns
into a full-blood Indian, he's usually
drunk, like last New Year's Eve
when our scattered family ate and drank
and sang together, firewater flowing.

Long ago I vowed not to drink
those waters that flame
me into feelings I yearn to shelve
forever — make us recall
why we should kill ourselves.

But just like New Year's —
when my reserved brother drank so much
he slung his arms around me, cried
I love you, you're still my little sister —

I can stumble back
to my younger self when only
alcohol could pry my tongue
from girlhood shamings,
silencings.

Yes, my brother, who teaches
the history of our Iroquois people
to school children, in suit and tie
survives his days — my brother
sometimes drinks

until he lives at Confederacy founding,
blood grown uncomplicated
in woods and meadows
and piney air.

If you go camping with us in May
I'll wear a breech cloth, do
my Indian dances for you
around the fire, he trip-danced
spring's preview with bowed legs.

Sure, I agreed, *I'll bring*
Native CDs for you to dance to,
because by now I'd broken
my vow – drinking
my own damned way
to being a full-blood.

And my silver-haired brother,
who never believed he was beautiful,
shouted, *I don't need any CDs*
to dance to. I've got my own Indian music
inside my head –

and my brother, the Indian brave,
war-whooped, *Do you know*
what it feels like? Do you?
When I was a boy I could fling
myself against a mountain, spread
my arms on Catskill earth, fly
as an eagle straight into her,
I was that close.

I wanted to howl back, *Yes,*
my brother, I know. It's okay.
But he was already singing
Karaoke with the rest of them.
And I, being the quiet one,

staggered outside
to cry forever
beneath the sober stars.

BUFFALO NICKEL MAKES RETURN

after a 63 year absence. Odd how happy I feel
when I read newspaper blurb next to photograph
of a buffalo called Cody. Ceremony *accompanied by*
Indian dancing, drum-beating and chanting, words swirl up
as Cody lowers dark head in Capitol Hill snow.

My sister gave me a buffalo nickel once,
inside a secret compartment in a tiny box.
Sometimes I pull it out, hold it in my hand,
the buffalo, the face of an Indian man, the nickel
color of rain. Strange, my happiness.

After all, the ones we dance for told us
someday we'd think like them, forget
our tribes, try to own the earth. Guaranteed
we'd believe nickels and dimes
could buy a better life than that one they stole.

So how is it when we caught their lies and
the genocide continues and we don't have jobs and our
children go hungry and our languages get lost and our sons
and daughters commit suicide, that 97 million newly minted
buffalo nickels make me feel a wild bliss,

as if from a secret compartment in the pine-box past
97 million buffalos might stampede back?

WHY I LOVE BEING AN INDIAN (for Erelene)

I can be grocery shopping in the Giant, rolling my cart down
the frozen food aisle, gathering frozen corn and Hagen Das Peach
Sorbet, when my cell phone that I swore I'd never get starts jingling its
joyous ring of song that always makes me want to jingle dance, and it's
my sister telling me about three nights ago, how she gazed up into sky
after the snow storm stopped and she had a vision, the clearing clouds
clustered into a Mohawk warrior's profile and tomahawk
above our Indian grandfather's house, and she watched in a trance
until the vision disseminated to make way for a few stars,
and I love this about being Indian, having a sister call me like this,
me stopping in my tracks under fluorescent lights in a grocery store,
grinning a giant of a smile as she tells me about a cloud warrior,
asking each other what that Sky Indian could mean,
looking forward to the cold delicate taste of peaches
like summer visions kissing my tongue later that winter night
and life's serious shoppers staring at me as if I've gone mad.

AFTER READING YOUR SNOW POEMS (for Martin Willitts)

2 a.m. rain flies like gold geese against garret window, water
wings lit up trembling from streetlights. Out there
wind chimes tinkle, jingle dance to wind carrying long,
low thunder laced with lightning. Often at this hour I
metamorphose into Japanese poetess, recall tea ceremonies
with Lady Murasaki behind rice paper screen. Tonight –
closed eyelids the only screen I know. Through this screen
green eyes re-read poems you've sent, your last letter –
after reading my snow poems you think *you* will write more
snow poems before the snow really arrives. Somehow
that vision comforts me – snow before winter, snow
in Indian summer, snow Technicolor with haikus
and Kyoto crystals and Zen mountains
that you can hold in origami hand before winter logjams
us into despair. Every year I am rapturous with first snowfall.
I buy plum wine to celebrate. I dance in the storm, fling
myself on whirling earth, open mouth wide to snow crystals
melting delicate songs into my tongue. When rain poured
down tonight, thunder rolled in, I thought the terrorists
had come again. I felt so lonely – I had no one to die with.
How I laughed in the darkness when it was only rain.
When I am a Japanese poetess, I can see noble court poets
beyond translucent screen I hide behind. They dream
of catching cranes flying across my kimono silk and
winter silk of my thighs. Tonight in America I see
you through eyelids – snow angel flying like a koan
across rice paper screen

ENCAMPMENT

At the airport terminal he told her to keep his sleeping bag.
After all, he'd be returning to live with her. He spoke quick
words about not crying. She didn't know who he meant
might cry. She said she was studying to be a tough broad.
They hugged, he flew off. She stumbled
to her car.

A few nights later she listened to summer rain
crying on street and roof. It thundered.
The cats hid somewhere.

She knelt next to the cardboard box
that held his sleeping bag, hands
pulling apart battered flaps. She
almost smiled at the pillow spotted
like leopard skin, unrolled the jungle
green bag across hardwood floor. Naked
she crawled in.

She clawed the starlight his body left behind.

MOON SEEING

After you left, I no longer could sleep on our garret bed.
Instead, I slept on the old bed you dragged into the living room –
we were too poor to buy a couch. Tonight I felt brave,
climbed the stairs to where we once held each other
against the night. When my marriage broke up
I nailed a card to bare wall: "Barn's burnt down,
now I can see the moon." My affair with you done
I re-read Masahide's words, slip
between burgundy sheets, satin
celestial fingers on my skin.

A quarter century ago I read how George Sand
wanted to be with just one man. Her wish turned into
many lovers. So she ooh la la'd, "Each lover
is a new education for me." Even then I suspected
my fate might be French. I couldn't keep away
from French films. Nights I dreamed in the language
and Jean Paul Belmondo licked me breathless
the way you did on our garret bed decades later –
your Asian mouth thicker than Jean's, your eyes
languorous eagles.

I stretch my flesh on the satins of memory
the way my Persian cat stretches hers.
January moon spills light through window.
My winter hair spills across your ghost
and his come-cries floating out into outer space forever.
I close eyes – smile. Have I not
grown more educated?

ONE GOOD INDIAN MAN

Lily-Lacks-an-Indian-Name drove her Indian car
across Susquehanna, rounded curve too fast, blues CD
blasting, Janis Joplin bellowing "One Good Man,"
Lily's Indian ass fancy dancing right off her seat,
fingers dancing off steering wheel. Yes,
Lily-Lacks-an-Indian-Name howled along
with dead Janis, flying west, winter sunset full
in her eyes, wailing her own version –
"One Good Indian Man."

Yeah, where was that man? Lily was dancing and flying
past massacres of 18th century Indian people near where
Susquehanna and Chenango Rivers flow into each other
like man and woman, spotted a cop in speed trap,
slowed down, nope, she didn't care about going
to white feminists' parties, knifing angry notches
in the belt she didn't wear. Lily-Lacks-an-Indian-Name
noticed an Indian man in deer hide robe hitchhiking
on roadside, a second warrior flashing the cop the bird. She

waved to the ghosts. Sun collapsing beneath western hills,
Janis massacring her lungs, Lily-Lacks-an-Indian-Name
flashed on autumn she saw Joplin sing, swig her Comfort
in between despair and desire. "One Good Indian Man," *damn*,
just *one* to ride fast, free, slow, wild as her Indian pony car,
just *one* like the old braves with the old love and the old eloquence
and the old trust. Janis, overdosed soon after far back September,
night flooding in, Lily-Lacks-an-Indian-Name kissing
frigid air, "Just One Good Indian Man, Just One."

BEAR MEDICINE (for William Meyers)

William, Cherokee man, friend, you told me
you had made something to protect me. You laughed
you were sending it "snail-mail" — and when it came
it would come as a surprise. "Let me know when it arrives,"
you teased through phone wires. "Then I'll explain it to you."
I have always been a woman who loves surprises, so
I laughed with you. That October the surprise arrived —
fringed turquoise pouch beaded with hoop of rainbow colors
hung from a strap braided like sweetgrass. Two tiny bears hung
black from suede blue; hint of amethyst glinted from strap.
Deep inside the pouch curled a bundle of turquoise cotton.
I lifted it from pouch's secret sky, cradled it on open palm —
unseen medicine inside humble cloth.

It was my birthday, day of my walking 52 years
on Mother Earth. I called to let you know
your surprise arrived. "I am Bear Clan," you said.
"That is your medicine pouch. Twin bears
will protect you, little sister. Bundle inside
is a medicine bundle. Use that to pray with. Use that
for healing. Keep it with you when the light of your heart
needs to be sheltered. Everything I placed within the bundle
has special meaning for me. Whenever you wish,
add what carries power for you."

William, my brother, my cousin, my friend,
I never unknotted the bundle until this winter of sub-zero days.
This winter that reminded me of how you used to say,
"The world is becoming more of the darkness, but you
are a dreamer woman and of the light."
This winter when I did not know if I could find
the sun inside myself anymore.
This February when I learned you had danced on
to another world.

William, you told me I could add to my medicine bundle.
But when I saw what you placed in it, my heart glowed with the beauty
of your delicate dreams for me. Cherokee man, you gave me a pouch
holding bear medicine, a secret sky, a medicine bundle
whose blue meanings my fingers have now touched.
What can I add — except wild weeping for that Indian country
we shall never have?

ROCK HARD

Whenever e-mails pop up with words
like "erection" and "penis enhancer,"
"Viagra" and "cum," I mark them *Junk*.

Once in awhile – like tonight
when if I weren't so tired I'd drive
to a mountainside to watch Perseids

flame down to fields no longer as lit
by fireflies – once in a very blue moon
I wonder who those faceless, bodiless

desperados are, penetrating my inbox
with premature spellings, flaccid grammar
and sticky run-on bullshit promises

reminding me of bad porno flicks
that could never make me wet
my buckskin thongs "all night long."

Who are they? Could I ever be rock hard
up enough to peddle herbal revolution
and 20 inch dicks? Imagining such ghosts

can make me sad when I press *Delete*
and – as on this night when I collapse
into bed with no benefit of sex aids or any

of Amerika's junk – feel the inside softness
of me, make love like that to the *deleted*, just me
soundless in a night of unseen meteors.

ROCK' N ROLL RAVENS

"They have to sing; if they didn't sing, everyone
would walk past, as if they were fences or trees"... Rilke

Raven was horny. Southern springs made Raven feel
this way. Actually, everything made Raven feel this way.
So Raven flapped and flew drunk with sex through
1950's Memphis streets. Raven hated the 'Fifties,
the sleeping cities, the sleepwalking people. Maybe
she'd have better luck in the poor section of town.
Maybe her hunt for a human with something
of Tupelo honey between his legs would find its match
in hungry alleys where wildness could still hide out.
Raven heard an angel's voice sing like a negro
about to be lynched. She dove toward the singing
and the guitar that twanged in crazy oneness with it.
Her beaded eyes sparkled to black diamonds.
Past an open window a boy with Raven's hair
and pants pegged snake-tight to skinny legs
was playin' that guitar. His upper lip curled
like a juicy caterpillar. Raven smacked her beak,
"Good eating!" The black rainbows of her wings
flapped themselves into Raven-haired Cherokee girl.
"Hi, my name is Moon Star," she managed to sound
like a typical bird. The teenager banged his guitar hard.
"Ah'm Elvis." His blue eyes smoke-signaled back.
Raven hopped over to him naked. "Well, Elvis,
your mother is nowhere to be seen. How would you like
to love me tender?" In no time Raven and Elvis
were playing each other like two fine guitars
until Raven howled like Coyote and Elvis got all
shook up. After that, Elvis never could stop
shaking his pelvis. The rest, as they say,
is Rock 'n Roll.

BURIAL (for Eric Schwartz)

Write your poems. Bury them deeply in the woods.
Maybe someone will find them someday —
and try to imagine what we lost. Eric Schwartz

Friend, tonight I am imagining choosing poems
for burial. Ever since we wrote to each other
about our Mother, beautiful Earth, and what we
humans have done, I am thinking of another funeral.
All night I have considered my poems, these only
children of mine, thinking of ways I shall roll
or crumple them up, poke them into emptied
wine bottles or once full jelly jars. And where will I
bury them? In what places might I do ceremony
over them, let fall sweet smelling tobacco to the ground
after the words are covered over with my sadness?

My brother, let us travel to Catskills
and I shall show you the country I grew up in,
mountains I am homesick for, Onteora, Land
in the Sky, where the stories descend from.
We can drive Route 17 before it's renamed
I-86, follow the trail of extinct panthers. Yes,
someday maybe a man of heart who wanders
as you do in the woods, finds bright mushrooms,
stands still so as not to frighten doe, will discover
the burial ground, feast on aged poems as on
the vintage wines and wild berry preserves
of better times.

My brother, my cousin, my friend, I can only imagine
that any survivor who imagines what we lost
will forgive us.

THE ONLY CEREMONY WE HAD LEFT TO US
(for Lance Henson, Ron Welburn
& Sara Littlecrow-Russell)

I am not going to pretend. The only ceremony
we had left to us was taking rides in a dented
Chevy on dirt roads no city slickers could find.
The only ceremony left to us was stopping
at a path we mountain Indians knew about,
stepping behind one another, hands brushing
the bent ferns. The ceremony never stolen
was walking a stony trail to a cliff, where
we made our stand with oaks, spruces, maples,
a few surviving hemlocks. I am not going to lie.
We still had a family, in some ways a tribe.
But our prayer was staring across valleys
at Catskill peaks answering us
with blue.

My brothers, once I dreamed
of Cheyenne stallions and Cherokee fire.
My sister, once I cried for Chippewa bear medicine
when they cut my tongue. Can I pretend otherwise?
The last ceremony left to me is riding
the broken horses of love off cliffs.

BIO:

Susan Deer Cloud is a writer of Blackfoot, Mohawk, Seneca heritage (Métis) who grew up in the Catskill Mountains. She is an alumna of Binghamton University where she has occasionally taught Creative Writing. Currently she is in MFA Fiction Program at UMass, Amherst.

Deer Cloud's other books of poetry are *The Broken Hoop* and *In the Moon When the Deer Lose Their Horns*. She is the editor of the multicultural anthology *Confluence*. She has also published poems, stories, and essays in numerous literary journals and anthologies – *Rosebud, Pembroke Magazine, To Topos, Ms, Many Mountains Moving, Sojourner, North Dakota Quarterly, Quarterly West, Arizona Quarterly, Mid-American Review, Paterson Literary Review, Negative Capability, Shenandoah, Prairie Schooner, Ladyfest*East Anthology, Sister Nations: Native American Women Writers on Community, A Nation Within: an Anthology of Native American Poetry, Listening to Water, the Susquehanna Watershed Anthology*, WPFW 89.3 FM Poetry Anthology (from Public Radio's "The Poet and the Poem"), *American Mixed Race: The Culture of Microdiversity, Out of the Catskills and Beyond: Literary and Visual Works by Catskill Writers and Artists*, and Penguin's *Unsettling America: an Anthology of Contemporary Multi-Cultural Poetry* and *Identity Lessons: Contemporary Writing About Learning to Be American*, among others.

Deer Cloud has received awards and special recognition in literary competitions for both her poems and stories (for instance, her poem "Tree" received first prize in the Allen Ginsberg Poetry Competition; her poem "Vincent Van Gogh Writes To Madame Calment From The Stars" was awarded second prize in *Negative Capability's* Eve of St. Agnes Poetry Competition; and two of her poems received Readers' Choice Award from *Prairie Schooner*). She is a recipient of a New York State Foundation for the Arts Poetry Fellowship, a Chenango County Council for the Arts Individual Artist's Grant, and is the founder of Binghamton Underground Poets, Wild Indians & Exuberant Others, Unc. (Unincorporated). Most recently she was awarded the National Endowment for the Arts Literature Fellowship in Poetry (2007).